In Our Life Time

100 Ideas, Thoughts & Observations for Today's World

David McGuigan

In Our Life Time
100 Ideas, Thoughts & Observations for Today's World

© 2015 by David McGuigan

ISBN: 978-0-9965920-0-0 paperback
978-0-9965920-1-7 ebook-epub
978-0-9965920-2-4 ebook-mobi

Library of Congress Control Number: 2015953311

All Rights Reserved Under International and Pan-American Copyright Conventions. No part of this book may be used or reproduced in any manner whatsoever without written permission except in the case of brief quotations embodied in critical articles or reviews.

Cover Illustration credit:
© Somchai Somsanitangkul | Dreamstime.com

Photo credits:
Monkey Feeding Tiger | Buzzfeed
p. 25 Family photo | Julie Irene Photography
p. 73 Diverse crowd around bright light | Caiaimage/Martin Barraud

Printed in the United States of America by
Mira Digital Publishing
Chesterfield, Missouri 63005

Dedication

To my wonderful children

and to all those who care

about making a real, meaningful

and positive difference in the world.

Contents

Dedication iii
Preface vii
Acknowledgements ix
Introduction xi

Peaceful Coexistence 1
Exploration & Discovery 13
Love 25
Environment 37
Collaboration 49
Leadership 61
Connectivity 73
Taking Action 85
Compassion 97
In Each of Us... 109
Post Script 121

    Author's Note 123
    Ten Additional Thoughts for My Children
    and the Children of the World 125
    Dave McGuigan 127
    My Daily Prayer 129

Preface

All the lessons we will ever need to learn,
all the wise words which one person can ever absorb,
have all been given.

People of monumental wisdom,
Profound Thinkers,
have come before us.

They have given us the clues,
the passion, the reasons,
the life lessons.

Now is it up to us,
Today's Leaders,
people from all walks of life …

who until today
—**This Moment**—
have sat on the sidelines.

We **can** make a real,
meaningful and measurable difference
In Our Life Time.

It is up to us,
to see the words, to hear the voices —
To Act.

Acknowledgements

I'd like to thank all the generous mentors in my life for your love, guidance, insight and wisdom.

I'd also like to express my deepest gratitude to Dr. Jill Prolman and Sylvia Mendoza for their support in bringing this book to life.

Introduction

I want to be someone who makes a difference in his lifetime.

I want to make a difference on a social front, on a humanitarian front and on an exploration front.

I want to see the human race establish lasting peace, find a cure for cancer and other diseases, and discover a new galaxy in which we can live, all *In Our Life Time*.

I want to see us learn to respect and encourage our fellow human beings while protecting our safety *and* our environment.

There are others who stand with me – believing that we can make a real, meaningful and measurable difference as individuals *and* change the world by harnessing the connective powers of cooperation and collaboration.

Through these dynamic efforts we become an unstoppable *Power Base* capable of achieving objectives once thought unattainable. These foundational steps forward are only "lofty" when we fail to focus on today and the opportunities right before us.

The timing is right. Our chance is now.

In Our Life Time.

Dave

Peaceful Coexistence

1

Nothing humankind has ever built will survive without *Peace*.

We will fail to achieve *Peace* without first establishing *Peaceful Coexistence*.

2

Our ability to find peace
and build peaceful coexistence
begins and ends
with our own deeds and actions.

Peaceful coexistence starts from within.

3

Humankind cannot allow
hatred, violence, ignorance and intolerance
to triumph over love, collaboration, cooperation
and peaceful coexistence.

Hate-focused organizations
are a cancer on society
and must be challenged
if the human race is to survive.

4

Fighting to *protect* peace,
wherever it exists, is fundamental.

Reconstruction of our communities,
and of society's progress,
will always be far more expensive and difficult
than protecting what we already have today.

5

The quickest way
for the world to experience total anarchy
is to allow for the disenfranchisement
of our youth.

6

Extremism on any front
— be it religious, financial, social or governmental —
stimulates hatred, mistrust, envy and apathy.

These ingredients are the breeding grounds
for violence and war.

7

Do not let anger, hostility, violence or fear *outwork* love, mercy, compassion and peace.

8

Accomplishments can be gained
— and self-satisfaction realized —
without taking away, or destroying,
the possessions of others.

9

There are no walls high enough,
nor moats deep or wide enough
to keep an enemy out.

The key to our security
is in finding peaceful and creative ways
to reach out and convert our enemy's objectives
into collective, common interests
whenever possible.

10

From a foundation of peace,
all possibilities for a better tomorrow
become reality for the human race.

Exploration & Discovery

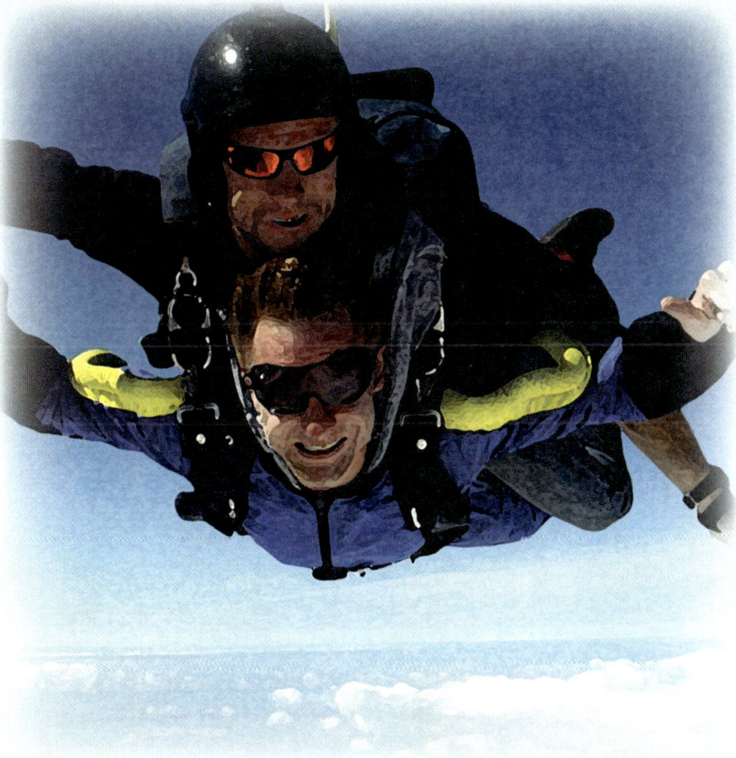

11

Our solar system is one of
200 billion solar systems
within the Milky Way Galaxy.

The Milky Way Galaxy is one of
100 billion galaxies
within the Universe.

Cosmologists and astronomers estimate
the Universe is comprised of
10 billion trillion stars
where an unlimited number of
solar systems exist.

When will we find the strength and commitment
to organize the wherewithal to
begin exploring this wonderful, unknown
world in which we live?

12

Everything we currently understand
— from our measured temperatures
to our interactive nature —
is guaranteed to be
ever-changing and unpredictable
all at the same time!

Exploration and *Discovery*
begins the moment
we step out our front door
each and every day!

13

Without *Exploration*
there can be no *Discovery*.

Without *Discovery*
we will cease advancing
the marvels of humanity.

14

We *limit* our ability to grow
every time we stop exploring, stop building,
stop challenging the unknown.

We *expand* our ability to grow
every time we risk, we challenge,
we explore and discover.

15

If we look far enough into the Universe,
we will discover things
we have never seen before.

If we look deep enough
into our own hearts and souls,
we will also discover things about ourselves
that we've never seen before.

***Self-exploration is
the greatest form of discovery!***

16

We're so busy chasing the *Street Signs* of life we often forget to focus on the *Celestial Signs* of our existence.

17

Every living organism *must* change and evolve if they are to survive and grow.

This includes *us*…the human race.

18

Humankind can learn
— and benefit from —
every single species on this planet.

19

If the caveman and cavewoman
never left the cave because of
the warmth of the fire and
the touch of the flesh,
where would we be today?

We must motivate ourselves
to step out of our own caves
and continue to explore the unknown.

20

When we stop being outwardly focused
we risk becoming stagnant,
petty and destructive.

Exploration and ***Discovery***
are the spiritual keys
to our continued evolution,
growth and development.

Love

21

Bring *Love* into every room that you enter…

22

Every single act of kindness…
be it big or small, random or calculated,
has a profound and meaningful impact
on humanity, the human condition
and the human race.

One random act of kindness
can convert an average day into many
extraordinary, significant and
memorable moments.

23

I do not wish to be known
for the jobs I have held
or the vocations I have practiced.

I want to be known
for the **Love** that I have shared,
the example I have set for others,
and the progress I've contributed to
In Our Life Time.

24

Love your children with all your might.

25

Extend love to others unconditionally
and on every occasion.

Grow from this great gift
every time it is extended to you.

26

The world benefits from every ounce,
every kilowatt, every gesture
of positive energy you can generate.

27

Love always starts and ends
with unconditional giving.

28

I found a new place to live today.
It's not too far away.

I've known of its location.
It's been with me each and every day.

It's not made of brick or mortar,
or even solid wood,
but it's a place that gives me shelter
like no other could.

I found a new place to live today.
It's right around the bend.
I plan to share it with everyone —
family, foe and friend.

I found a new place to live today.
My move was very smart.
For now I have everything,
because I'm living from my heart.

29

Reach *deep* into your heart
and find the courage and love
it takes to live a full, positive
and productive life.

30

Love is the *glue* that binds us together.

Love is the *fabric* that weaves together our human continuum.

Environment

31

Live where your community *fights* to protect your air, water, land and general welfare.

32

The most important environment
to protect and invest in is your own.

Feed and exercise your body, mind,
spirit and soul daily!

33

The existing power bases
— *government, money, military and religion* —
have tremendous influence over our
day-to-day existence.

Know them well and speak out
when they disparage the world
in which you live.

34

We are the earth's custodians.

Remember to leave our **Global Campsite** cleaner and in better condition than how you found it.

35

Stay connected to nature
and protect its richness,
for the health of our natural habitat
is the foundation from which we live.

36

We will build a better tomorrow by investing in
The Five Pillars of Progress:

Peaceful Coexistence

Economic Engagement

Environmental Reinvestment

Human Dignity

Exploration and Discovery

37

In environments where
inclusion and opportunity exist,
goodness will flourish and persist.

38

Reuse, recycle and respect every resource you are given.

39

Electronics are humankind's greatest addiction.

Unplug periodically and connect yourself with Mother Nature.

40

If humanity is going to
add value to the Universe,
we will need to build sustainable foundations
that last for millions of years…
and act in ways that push the human race
beyond *Low Earth Orbit*.

Collaboration

41

A single note on a piece of paper
is not music.
It takes many notes,
organized and arranged,
to make music.

Collaboration is humanity's orchestral score!

42

We are at our greatest
when we reach beyond ourselves,
when we recognize that our common interests
are far more important
than our differences.

43

Our individual strengths are amplified by our collective capabilities.

44

Our progress is predicated
on the fact that others
— either those before us or those with us today —
have been willing to work together,
sacrificing for a common good
while contributing toward
a better tomorrow for all.

— 45 —

We work together to make great things happen.

We stand together to defend them.

46

Learn the difference between
Having a Position and *Having a Perspective*.

A *Position*, while principled,
is limiting in its collaborative capabilities.

A *Perspective* allows for
unlimited collaboration and growth.

47

Collaboration requires a common motivation — be it altruistic, materialistic or practical.

Whenever possible, find — and build — on common ground.

48

On Planet Earth we have ourselves
and we have each other.

Alone, we cannot survive.
Together, we can thrive and grow.

49

Extremes cause tension.

Collaboration creates harmony.

50

Collaboration requires sacrifice, diligence, dedication and determination.

Collaboration requires measured progress and identifiable success.

Collaboration requires inclusion, flexibility and patience.

Collaboration is the foundation in which the ultimate fate of humanity rests.

Leadership

51

***Look Around*...**

for there is need everywhere.

***Be Strong*...**

for the world needs your leadership,
love and support.

***Never Doubt*...**

that you can make a difference.

52

You don't need to be *great* in order to be good, but you do need to be *good* in order to advance great accomplishments.

53

The future of this planet,
the future of the human race,
starts with each of us.

Be a visionary and voice for the world!

54

You cannot change the past,
but you can positively influence the future
by being *present* each and every day.

55

Even collective courage needs leadership.

Our greatest sin is to do nothing...

56

Leadership is being once removed
but twice as close.

Empowering others is the strongest form
of true leadership.

57

Seek out and enroll

a ***Coalition of the Willing***

then build

a ***Foundation for Progress***

which others can follow.

58

You will never scare good people away
with the truth.

You need not contrive in order to thrive,
to succeed and lead!

59

Balancing human celebration
with contribution and leadership
is a *magic* that requires
constant vigilance and regular adjustment.

60

Action always get attention.

Find something positive where you can
make a difference —
then make a difference!

Connectivity

61

We live in a unique and
extraordinary time in human history —
where, through human enlightenment
and global connectivity,
a handful of well intentioned,
passionate and dedicated souls
can change the fate and future
of the human endeavor forever.

62

Individual Enlightenment takes root when we become aware of who we are, understand the context of our existence, and grasp the importance of *purpose* and *meaning*.

63

We are at our greatest when we combine
the intellectual and spiritual powers
of our individual nature
with the unlimited strengths
of our collective capabilities.

64

What do seven billion people
living on a tiny rock
in a vast ocean of unknown
have in common?

EVERYTHING!

Our continued, evolving connectivity
binds **all of us**
to a common future
and a common fate.

65

It's fun to be *Facebook*™ *Famous*!

Imagine what the future looks like when we use our connectivity to make the world a better place!

66

If I walk alone every day, I may gain clarity, but lack connectivity.

Our global connectivity provides us with access to intellectual and physical energy which allows for individual *and* collective growth as we've never seen before.

Get plugged into the **Global Connectivity Grid** and let the juices flow!!!

67

In every garden there are a few flowers that resonate in color, scent and beauty.

Global Human Enlightenment starts with your own daily Brilliance.

Shine Bright every day for the world to see!

68

With the power of our words,
with well-organized and collective thought,
we have the strength of a thousand armies.

69

Beyond the Power Bases of
Government, Money, Military and Religion,
there is a new, rapidly emerging
5th *Power Base*
and it is *us*
— individuals from all walks of life —
bound by our common circumstance
and purpose.

We
— you and I —
are the 5th *Power Base*.

We are the solution
to today's complex problems
and the guardians of
tomorrow's unlimited opportunities.

70

Consciousness leads to awareness …

Awareness leads to responsibility …

Responsibility leads to action …

Action leads to connecting people of common interest everywhere…

Taking Action

71

I <u>can</u> make a difference …

I <u>will</u> make a difference …

I <u>am</u> making a difference …

We are always just two steps away from true contribution.

72

Believe in the basic premise that we ***can*** make a difference if we're simply willing to ***Act***.

73

A single positive act
can change the world forever.

74

A wise person is one who can see the greater perspective.

A hero is one who acts on it.

75

Good intentions without execution is nothing more than wishful thinking.

76

If we approach every day
only to self-satisfy
we will lose as a society
and as the human race.

Send yourself into service every day
to make a positive, real,
meaningful and measurable
difference.

77

Don't look away.

Don't mask reality
through distraction or addiction.

Look straight at the needs of the world
and step forward to do your part.

There is no such thing as a partial commitment.

*If we are truly going to make a difference
we must act and we must act now.*

78

The toughest part about addictions?
Stopping.

The toughest part about achieving significant milestones?
Starting...and not stopping.

79

Be the synergistic bonding agent that binds people, actions and activities together.

80

When all is said and done,
you and I have the chance to leave a legacy —
to make a real and meaningful impact
in our lifetime **and** for generations to come.

Compassion

81

As is the case with our physical existence, promoting *circulation* within our societal ecosystem is also essential.

The world needs our generosity in order to maintain a successful circulatory nature.

82

The measure of any good human being
can be found in their willingness
to share with others…

to give without restriction or reward,
to love and give unconditionally.

Being *in service* means
never looking for, or expecting,
anything in return.

83

How do we define **Community**?

Is it the block we live on?
The neighborhood we reside in?
The city, province or state?

It is time for us to realize
that we are all part
of the same global community.

A neighborhood in which
every neighbor and every citizen
has the opportunity to have access to
the same basic human rights and benefits
as everyone else.

84

Providing opportunity to every human being
is not an added burden to
the world's financial structure.

Involving every single human being
in the world's socio-economic system
only strengthens our ability
to grow the value proposition
which we are all a part of.

85

I hear all the voices.
I see all the choices.
I know the difference.

I start *today* to build
a better tomorrow for all.

86

It is unacceptable
for a civilization as advanced as ours
to allow hunger, poverty, disease and ignorance
to exist anywhere on Planet Earth.

*Let's identify and align humanity's needs
with our abundant global resources!*

87

Financial and economic systems
know no prejudice —
only the people who administer them do.

Society is at its best when
cooperation and collaboration thrive,
and when recognition and reward
are abundant.

88

Do not be afraid to share of yourself,
to give at all times and at any moment.

The ability to be selfless, caring and uninhibited
in your expressions and actions
are at the core of personal
and social growth.

89

We advance the ***human condition***
when we share what we have
— materially, intellectually and spiritually —
with those without.

We advance the ***human endeavor***
when we learn to work together
to the benefit of the common good.

90

In some places on our planet,
people feel fortunate to find,
and use over and over again,
a simple plastic fork.

In our society,
we use, then throw away,
that plastic fork
without thinking twice about it.

As you collect and give of your benefits,
be neither reckless nor ruthless.

Be generous with others,
for we take nothing with us
and gain little in life
except in the gifts
which we leave behind.

In Each of Us...

91

Be true to yourself.

Be honest with the world.

92

Being in service every day
is the easiest way
to wipe your troubles
and problems away.

93

You don't have to turn your world upside down in order to help the world stay right side up!

94

Shine Bright Every Day!

Never let external factors
extinguish your beautiful brilliance.

95

Why settle for average
when you can have extraordinary?

The signs are all around us —
signs of greatness, brilliance and capability.

These are not stop signs.

They are the signs of encouragement
— to accelerate and grow —
to reach far beyond the norm
to new heights of expectation
and accomplishment.

96

"It's the twig that trips the elephant."

The little actions and judgements in daily life matter as much as the big ones.

97

Think Small…Be Small.
Think Big…Be Big!

Every moment in life is a precious opportunity for unlimited learning, discovery, contribution and growth.

98

Tomorrow is a million miles away
when you make as much as you can
out of today!

*Challenge life to its fullest and be passionate
about everything good that is right before you.*

99

Stop and take a moment for yourself.

Find your voice and meet your soul.

We are inherently good,
and our goodness is the secret
to a better tomorrow.

100

One powerful candle can light the way
for a hundred willing souls.

A hundred willing souls
can impassion an entire generation.

An impassioned generation
can change humanity's fate and future forever.

We are each that powerful light
that shines bright for generations to come.

Post Script

Author's Note

Dear Readers:

In Our Life Time started out as a letter to my four children, an effort to share with them my beliefs, as well as my hopes and wishes for them as life unfolds.

We are all part of the **Human Continuum** — a never-ending movement of humanity that allows each generation the opportunity to make this Planet a better, more peaceful place today and enhance the long-term chances for the human race. The concept is not so far-fetched. It starts with you and me.

Each of us — no matter our age, geographic location, ethnicity or socio-economic circumstance — can make a difference. Like an orchestral score, we can be seen as individual notes that, when pulled together, produce amazing music. In a compassionate yet powerful way, we can step out of our comfort zones to make measurable and sustainable contributions.

I hope you have found at least one idea, thought or observation within these pages that has called to your spirit, to your soul, to your being. I encourage you to take action from the words provided by ***In Our Life Time***. This simple step between the two of us is the momentum that humanity needs to survive, thrive and grow.

Visit www.inourlifetime.net and let me know which chapter — which idea, thought or observation — resonates most with you so we can collaborate and grow a better tomorrow for all.

Thank you for joining me in making a measurable difference *In Our Life Time*.

Dave

Ten Additional Thoughts
for My Children and the Children of the World

1. Life is the greatest gift you will ever be given. What you do with it is the fundamental question essential to you and all those around you. Treat life as the unique, extraordinary and precious gift that it is.

2. When unsure, ask for guidance.
   When in trouble, ask for help.
   When confident, share yourself with others.

3. Think twice about everything you put into your body. Avoid addictions and distractions as much as possible and give what you can, when you can, toward making the world a better place for all.

4. Never stop thinking about those less fortunate.

5. Split your time between giving and growing. You *and* the world will be better for it!

6. We are becoming less connected with the earth because we allow **society** to deliver all of our needs. Stay connected to nature and protect its richness and its health. Without it, we have nothing.

7. The key to our future is in finding ways to safeguard the values of peace, love and hope until they are stronger than our destructive tendencies.

8. External trappings may motivate humankind, but it is what's inside us that drives the human endeavor. Lead with your heart.

9. Work hard to improve yourself and be open to growth and change. ***Don't let your shortcomings become your long suit.***

10. Every random and calculated act of kindness makes the world a better place. It strengthens and brightens the very fabric of humanity and the human race. Give *love* — and find those who will provide you with *love* — for it will make a difference in the world around you.

Dave McGuigan

Friends and associates know Dave as a **Conceptual Architect**. He has a knack of taking ideas that don't exist and framing them so that others can see the possibilities of what can be.

Dave is an idea enthusiast who loves to give birth to new ideas, concepts, products and initiatives, especially those that can help make the world a better place.

Born in Detroit and raised in Ann Arbor, Michigan, Dave has had the opportunity to travel the world and study with wonderful thinkers from all walks of life. He is inspirited by those willing to find and use their voice in an effort to make a positive difference for all.

Life's professional journey has seen Dave make significant contributions in sports and sports marketing, cause-related marketing, retailing, non-profit organizational development, and in the advancement of stem cell manufacturing and treatments.

Known for his "McGuiganisms", Dave uses unique expressions and phrases that help capture an idea or routine in order to create an easy-to-understand, 'Universal Language'.

A resident of Del Mar, California, Dave dedicates his time to his family and friends — and toward advancing ideas that may help the world become a better place for all living creatures for hundreds of generations to come.

My Daily Prayer

Let there be peace on earth.

Let every man and woman
find food for their stomach,
shelter for themselves and their family,
and enough opportunity so that
there is hope for the future.

And let us work with all living things
so that we may be
better guardians of the Planet today,
and so that we may become
citizens of the Universe tomorrow.

To these things I pledge my heart and soul.